Resilience

7 Keys to Bounce Back: The Power to Press Forward

Dr. Dara M. Lemite

Resilience: The Power to Bounce Back
7 Keys to Press Forward in Life

Copyright © 2017 Dr. Dara M. Lemite

Unless otherwise indicated, all Scripture quotations are taken from the King James Version of the Bible.

ISBN 10: 0692913351
ISBN 13: 978-0-692-91335-2

Book Cover & Design by OnPath Graphics

Printed in the United States of America

Dedication

To my son, Matthew, you're one of the many reasons, I had to "bounce back." I pray that you will know that God has an awesome plan for your life no matter the challenges you may face. God has truly blessed me with an amazing son! I love you more than words can say!

To my Mom and Dad, who've always supported me, loved me, and encouraged me to press forward in spite of the challenges I faced several years ago. You both have been such a pillar of strength to me. I thank God for you two every day! There are not enough words to say or show the lasting impact you have on my life. I am eternally grateful for you both.

Table of Contents

Introduction

The Word says that we are "more than conquerors" (Romans 8:37). That means we were created to overcome and outlast any challenge. Jesus never promised that we would not have troubles. In fact, He said, "I have told you these things, so that in Me you may have peace. In this world, you will have trouble. But take heart! I have overcome the world" (John 16:33).

Since Jesus overcame the world, we can overcome the world, too. I truly believe by learning how to become resilient and pressing forward in faith, you will overcome any challenge you may face in life.

According to Merriam-Webster, the definition of resilience is, *"an ability to recover from or adjust easily to misfortune or change."* I believe resilience is feeling the hurt and pain of something, processing what happened, and having the resolve to move on and move forward with your life. When you are resilient you don't get stuck in the past. You take the lessons learned with you and move into greater which is everything that God has for you.

Imagine you're living the life you envisioned. What does that look like? Part of being resilient is knowing that whatever you've come out of, or whatever has happened to you be it tragic, discouraging, or disheartening, you will come through it and not look like what you have been through. Another part of being resilient is having a vision for your life. Imagine your life grander and greater than where you are presently and push towards that. Knowing that whatever your mind can see, you can physically have it. This is true because the Bible says, "For as he thinks in his heart, so is he" (Proverbs 23:7 NKJV).

God puts dreams and visions in our hearts, because He has great plans for us (Jeremiah 29:11). However, in order to realize those dreams and see them come to pass, we will have to learn how to become resilient, overcome obstacles, and move forward into all that God has for us.

After you go through something, how do you bounce back? I wrote this book because this question was asked too many times by people who suffered while in relational, financial, health, and other challenges of life. What are the appropriate steps to take to move forward after a crisis?

In this book, you will learn practical tools on how to become resilient and apply it to any obstacle you may face in life.

Chapter 1

Your Purpose is Greater Than Your Pain

"And we know that all things work together for good to those who love God, to those who are the called according to His purpose" (Romans 8:28 NKJV).

My former bible study teacher, Vivian Allen, used to say, "The breaking of you, is the making of you". To be where God wants you to be, you will face some trials and tribulations. Everyone at some point will face challenges in life. When you are in Christ, you know that God's purpose for you is greater than the pain you may be presently facing. As the Scripture says, "All things work together for your good". This is when we must trust God. We may not know how, why, or when, but this is the time our faith should kick in as it pushes us forward.

As Pastor Rick Warren once said, "God wants you to learn something. Every storm is a school. Every trial is a teacher. Every experience is an education. Every difficulty is for your development." I also believe that God doesn't waste our hurts. When we go through painful experiences, we learn, grow, and become better than we were before.

After going through a failed marriage, I had to learn how to bounce back. A lot of my identity was centered around my role as a wife. Once I realized that my marriage was done, it was actually over before it was over, lol: however, I had to learn how to rebuild myself. If I didn't learn how to restore myself, I would have stayed in the deepest despair, and depression. At the time, I felt like a complete failure and a total loser.

While being resilient, you also should be able to take the fall, the harshness, and bounce back from everything. Let's use a handball for example. When I was in high school, I used to go to the park and play handball with my friends. Playing handball requires the players to take the handball and bounce it against the wall and then it bounces back to you, but before it bounces back to the players, it takes a hard hit against the wall. To gain resiliency, you're going to go through some harsh times. You will go through some challenges, disappointments, and some things that will upset you beyond human reasoning. It may even leave you feeling confused like, "Why is this happening to me?" But, in that challenge, in that hard time, that moment of despair, you start to realize that there has got to be a *message* in the madness. You realize that God has a bigger plan for you. Then, you start to rebuild yourself and become resilient.

A friend of mine once said, "Everyone wants a breakthrough, but no one wants to be broken." You will go through some things as you fulfill your God-ordained purpose. Every day is not going to be a bed of roses. There will be ups, downs, and at times, you may not like it. This should be a reminder to you that you must press through. Jesus himself said that there will be troubles. The most amazing thing is that because of Him, we can face our troubles head on, push through it, and persevere. Please realize that you are not here on this earth by accident. Everything that happened to you is working out for a greater purpose in you. The awesomeness of God is that He will use it for your greater good. He will use any and everything to get us to our appointed destination. As a believer, your life is not your own. You are called and set apart for the Maker's use.

Truly Let Go, and Let God

A portion of becoming resilient is knowing that you don't have it all figured out. Sometimes in life, we don't have all the answers and that's okay. This is where we must trust God for every area of our lives. There may be things in your life that you haven't quite figured out yet, but know that God has a plan and a purpose for you. When we trust God for every area of our lives, He will reveal His plan for us according to Jeremiah 29:11. The Bible states, "Call to me and I will answer and tell you great and unsearchable things you do not know" (Jeremiah 33:3 NIV). In my own life, I realize that I must trust God. There are things in my life, that I haven't spoken to anyone but God, and I'm trusting Him to make the paths straight to reveal things to me which leave me unsure. There is a common saying, "Let go and let God," but how many of us are *really letting go and letting God* do the work that He needs to do in our lives? When you can release the reins over your life and put your life in God's hands, there's a peace that will come over you that surpasses all human understanding. Also, as you trust Him, He will reveal His plan for you; His divinely orchestrated plan for your life. You see man's thinking is finite, but God's thinking is infinite, His wisdom is pure (James 3:17). And in His Word, it says that His ways are higher than our ways, and His thoughts are higher than our thoughts (Isaiah 55:9).

Now, I'm not going to say that this is going to be easy. For those of us who would like to be in control of everything and every area of our lives, it's kind of hard to relinquish that control; however, when you know that you are putting your life in the hands of The One who created you, you will begin to understand that His plan is far greater than the plan that you can ever imagine for yourself. One of my favorite scriptures, says that "It will all work out for your good." (Romans 8:28). No matter what happens throughout the course of our lives, in the end it will all work out for our good. Once again, we must trust God through the process while knowing that He will take us every step of the way.

I am a very friendly person by nature, and quite often people tell me that my life appears to be so easy. They also say that I don't seem to have troubles. I can't even count the amount of times people have said everything in your life seems so perfect and fine. "You're always happy, you're always smiling, always upbeat," They commented. But, there's a common saying, "Not every smiling face is a happy one". I am here to tell you that letting go and letting God is truly a daily process. Sometimes, it's even a minute by minute process. Sometimes, I'm like "Lord what are you doing in my life?" Then sometimes it seems that there are unanswered questions or things that I don't quite understand. Therefore, this is where I must trust God. I truly believe as we trust God, He will reveal His plan for us bit by bit. When I think about His process for our lives, I'm reminded of a puzzle. If you will, picture a puzzle. It can be a 50-piece puzzle or 100-piece puzzle, either way it has a lot of pieces. As you're assembling the puzzle, you remember to take it piece by piece. So, this is similar to the process with our lives as we have to take it by piece and step-by-step allowing God to complete this masterpiece we call life.

The most comforting thing is that when we truly let go and let God, we place our lives in the palm of His hands knowing that He will work it out for our good. We may not have all the answers. I don't think any human on this earth does. There are some things that we may not even figure out in this lifetime. There are some things that we may be able to find out when we cross over into eternity, but as we are here on this earth, we must trust God like in Psalms 138:8, which states, "He will fulfill His purpose for us". As I said previously, His plan and purpose far exceeds anything that we can ever think and imagine. How do I know this you may ask? Because in His Word He says that "He will give us above all that we ask or think." (Ephesians 3:20).

When we truly let go and let God, we go from being pitiful to powerful. We go from settling to being secure in ourselves. We go from tribulations to triumphs!

God is Able

When things look contrary to what your spirit believes, this is the time you should look through the eyes of faith. As believers, we have to understand that God operates in the spiritual realm. Man looks at the one dimension, but God is infinite, or multi-dimensional. God is infinite in His wisdom, His power, and His authority.

Any opposition that you may be experiencing is a clear indicator that you're pushing toward something different. Something that will help you ascend to the next level! Stay focused, stay the course, and know that God's got you! Others may think it looks easy, but they have no idea that you may be battling within yourself *every* day. When you're on the road to resilience, it may seem at times that it is an uphill battle. During this fight, be resolved in your spirit that God has a bigger and better plan for you. Although life is not perfect, we serve an awesomely perfect God! God truly honors those who honor Him. When your faith is stronger than your circumstances, that's when you become unstoppable! God's plan for you is greater than your present. He will fulfill His purpose for you (Psalm 138:8). Everything that you are walking through, He will turn it around for your good. You are more than a conqueror! This means you will win and overcome!

Please understand, what you do know about God is stronger than what you don't know about your future. It costs to follow Jesus. Once again, I am not going to say it will be easy, but it will be worth it. As for me, I have resolved within my own spirit that I will follow God to the best of my ability. We are called to be ambassadors of Christ (2 Corinthians 5:20).

Finding Peace Within

On your journey to becoming resilient, there is a mission to find peace within. Deep within, God has given you great gifts and talents. Sometimes in the noise and clutter of the world it is hard to find peace. I truly believe when you get in your quiet space and listen to the unction of the Holy Spirit, you will find peace. Therefore, His word says that you will have peace that surpasses all human understanding. On the road to resilience, it's important to find your peace and what makes you happy. All of us have been given the greatest gift--the gift of life. We all have been given the gift of 24 hours. It's up to you to decide whether you will make use of the time you are given wisely. On this journey of becoming resilient, you will have to find what makes you happy and brings you joy.

One day, I was sitting in my classroom after school, and a student came in to pick up her saxophone. My room was totally quiet as I was sitting at my desk writing. She asked me, "Do you ever get lonely?" She then elaborated that it was so quiet in the room that she would feel lonely. I quickly replied, "No, I enjoy the peace, and at times, I enjoy the noise". It's all about finding balance in your life. You see you must enjoy being you and enjoying your own company. When people say they don't like to be alone or they're frightened to be by themselves because it makes them upset or down, I believe it's because they don't have that certain peace within. They may feel insecure about themselves. But when you have peace within, you will find that you like yourself and you may begin to revel and enjoy your quiet time.

Keys to Remember

- There is a purpose for your pain
- Your pain will push you to your purpose
- Trials come to strengthen you
- Your faith needs to be stronger than your circumstances.
- You are more than a conqueror

- Cast your cares on God
- God has given you great abilities and talents
- Your purpose is greater than your present

Chapter 2

FIND MEANING EVERYDAY

*"I would have lost heart, unless I had believed
That I would see the goodness of the Lord in the land
of the living" (Psalm 27:13 NKJV).*

Several years ago, I remember having to go
back to my parents' house, and feeling like a
complete failure. My marriage was over. Done.
Nothing. Nada. Zilch. I remember thinking to myself,
what now? Lord, what am I going to do? I felt like my
life was totally over. Not only was I going through a
divorce, I ended up being a single mom to a 6-month-
old baby.   The very thing I never wanted to happen to
me in life, did. I was now left with the task of raising
my son alone. I felt empty, hurt, angry, bitter, and a
whole range of negative emotions flooded my mind.
My thoughts and overthinking began to overwhelm
me.   I thought to myself, but I am a *good* woman, this
isn't supposed to happen to me! I played by the rules.
I was a loving, faithful, and dutiful wife. How could
this happen to me? How could he step out on me?

Doesn't he see how good of a woman I am? How can he embarrass me like that? Why did he make me look like a fool? A thousand questions with no plausible answers engulfed my mind rapidly. I remember at one point being angry with God. And questioned Him, "How can you let this happen to me? Divorce is not in my family line. No one is divorced in my family." Except me. I felt like a black sheep. Thank God no one ostracized me, but I felt like I was the topic of conversation at dinner tables, across my extended family. I told you my thoughts were overwhelming!

At that point, I remember questioning everything I knew, or at least I thought I knew, and God was one of them. I was like "I'm a praying, and fasting woman, this *isn't* supposed to be *my* portion. This is some *mess*, that's supposed to happen to someone else." I said this as if I was exempt from troubles or better than the next person. At one point, I could feel my head and eyes rolling, too. I was all out of sorts. I truly went through. I started to become resentful and **hated** seeing happily married couples especially those who consisted of women who I thought was unworthy of love and didn't appreciate their husbands as they should.

"You're not the first woman and you won't be the last"

Those were the very words my Dad said when he and my mom sat with me at the kitchen table. As harsh as those words were, it was also comforting at the same time. It was good for me to know that I was not the only woman who went through a divorce. In life as we go through troubles, we automatically think we're the only ones going through such troubles. We often don't realize that everyone has troubles in life. If you live long enough, there will be some challenges to face and overcome. My sisters and brothers, we live in a fallen world. Therefore, things will take place that are not so favorable at times. Therefore, we need to press into God even more and trust Him to see us through. Remember, Jesus said that we would have troubles (John 16:33). But, the trouble does not come to last or overtake us. As believers, we were created to overcome any challenge. Part of being resilient is learning how to bounce back through the adversities of life. A key characteristic of resilient people is that they have suffered great challenges but also endured. You may bend, but you won't break. God is with you through every trial that you may face or are facing in life. He knows how to get you through it. *"Cast your cares on the Lord and he will sustain you; He will never let the righteous be shaken"* (Psalm 55:22 NLT).

Be Present in the Moment

Another characteristic of resilient people is the fact that they know how to be present in the moment. People who are resilient are not concerned with looking back, but more concerned about looking ahead. The awesome thing about God is that He will never leave you the same. The trials in life come to elevate us and move us forward in our life's purpose.

It is so important to take time and appreciate the progress you have made. Sometimes we get so caught up in what is wrong in our lives that we forget to focus on what is right and what is working. As the saying goes, "Stop and smell the roses". Look around you. Think about the goodness of the day. The very fact that you are still here in the land of the living is something to rejoice about. Think about the people God has placed in your life. Be it your spouse, children, family members, friends, co-workers, etc. We all have something to be grateful for.

I recall the times, when I was going through my divorce and work became my solace. My co-workers/friends do not know the extent of how their smiles and caring words helped me to get through. I remember attending a conference, and the pastor said, "Sometimes, we are looking for the spectacular, and miss the supernatural". God can take moments that are ordinary and make them extraordinary. According to Philippians 1:6, *God will finish the work that He started in you.*

Resilient people also know that there is something to learn from what they went through. While going through these challenging times, I kept looking for the message in the madness. I truly believe God does not allow things to just happen to us. There is always a reason why things occur in our lives.

Stay in Your Lane

A lot of times we try to rush ahead of God thinking He is not moving fast enough. But, when you quiet your mind and let the Holy Spirit speak to you, you will realize you are just where you need to be. God's timing for our lives is perfect. When we put God first, and the cares of this world last, He will bring more clarity and understanding that you have ever known. His word says, *"In all thy ways acknowledge Him, and He will direct your paths"* (Proverbs 3:6). When you acknowledge God, and allow Him to lead your life, He will take you on paths you've never seen and known.

I believe a lot of our pain in life comes when we put high expectations onto people instead of God. Please understand, man will fail you continuously but God never fails. Even though we may not understand His ways, God is *always* consistent. He's not going to change up on you. It's been said that people change their moods like they change their underwear, and one of the hardest lessons I had to learn in life, and still learning, is that what you do for others does not mean that they will necessarily reciprocate. This is where you will have to be resilient. You must be able to bounce back from the disappointments and hurt from other people.

When you stay in your lane, there are no rivals. When you're in your lane, you are right where God has called you to be. An example that comes to mind is when God brought flying back to my remembrance.

I have flown many times before, but I am reminded when the pilot announces, "We are about to cruise at an altitude of 32,000 feet." Another example that came to mind is your car's cruise control. When the car is placed on cruise control, you do not have to worry about accelerating or decelerating. You don't have to speed ahead, press the brake to slow down, or hold back because you're right where you need to be. While you're operating on cruise control, it's going to be effortless yet graceful. There isn't any pressure, stress, worry, fear or any of those negative emotions. When you're operating and staying in your lane, the lane that God has for you, you will operate with so much grace. I truly believe a lot of our stress in life comes from when we take our eyes off what God has called us to do and start to look at what others are doing. It's so important to not allow the distractions of this life to deter you from your God-given purpose. Another part of being resilient is not allowing the distractions, hurts, and the negative things that has happened to us to hold us back from pressing forward into everything that God created us to be.

According to the Merriam-Webster, the definition of grace is simple elegance or refinement of movement as believers. As believers, the word grace means, "the free and unmerited favor of God." When we stay in our lane, God gives us the grace to continue in everything that we need to do. He gives us the grace to press forward in ministry. He gives us the grace to write a book, start a business, raise a family, and a whole host of things.   Everything we want and need is found by having a relationship with God. And even in His word, He says His grace is sufficient for us (2 Corinthians 2:19).

Run your Own Race

One of the things we must realize is that we come into this world alone. That means we will also exit this world, in this form, by ourselves. Every one of us have been given a divine assignment by God. It is up to us whether we will fulfill that assignment. We should as the Bible says, "Set our face like a flint (and run our own race. Not looking to the right, or to the left, but pressing forward into everything that God has for us." (Isaiah 50:7),

Part of bouncing back is learning how to stay in your own lane. Too often we get caught up in other people's lives or drama and not focused on our own race and purpose for God. When you realize you're a unique and original design, you will move from feeling inadequate to having a resolve and determination to push through and push forward.

Another key to resilience is knowing that God has an appointed season and timing for your life. So many people live with regrets while so many people live without trying, and giving up. What I want you to understand is this: you will not leave this earth until you have accomplished everything that God has created and designed for you to be and become. I cannot impress it upon your soul enough to trust God's timing for your life. Therefore, the Scripture says my times are in your hands (Psalm 31:15). We need to do what we can do, and God will do what we cannot do. This is why the Word says, "I can do all things through Christ who gives me strength" (Philippians 4:13). I remember one day finishing a band rehearsal with my students. When the students left, I put my flute together and I started to practice on the stage. I remember loving the sound of the flute and the acoustics in the room, and how it seemed that my flute sound emanated and resonated throughout the whole auditorium. Suddenly, I had a flashback of my days at Hofstra University. I remember how I was filled with such anxiety, or should I say, performance anxiety. I remember how my stomach would fill with knots at the thought of performing, and I couldn't understand how something I loved so much was causing me so much fear. My heart would beat so fast, I thought it would leap from my chest! My palms would get sweaty, my knees were shaking. I was grappled with fear; frozen, if you will. While going to a band rehearsal, I remember my mom driving me up to the music building as I looked at her and said, "I can't get out of the car". I was beyond nervous. I had such anxiety because I felt that I didn't match up. I felt as if I wasn't as good as the other flautists. I felt that I didn't deserve to be in the band. I thought that I was not worthy of being anywhere in the flute section. My mind told my body to just go home. You're not good enough. How did you even get into the band in the first place? Various thoughts like these filled my mind like a flood. At that moment, I began to talk down to myself.

As I said earlier, we have to run our own race. God has our time and our season already predestined. There is no need to compare yourself to others. You are where you're supposed to be. Sometimes we have to get out of our own way. We can be our own worst enemy at times. We should have freedom from fear to truly walk into everything that God has for us.

Put it in Perspective

When you become resilient, situations may come, but it will "bounce" off you. This happens when you know God's purpose for your life. You won't have time for any games. During this next half of my life, I plan to fully *go in* with God's purpose for me. There are certain things I want to accomplish before I leave this earth and most importantly, I want to make sure I leave a legacy for my son. I want to make sure that my son will be fully taken care of and want for nothing and be financially free. I want him to be able to fully use all the resources afforded him so that he can fully live out the call of God on his life.

This next half of my life, I decree and declare will be the best half of my life. I want to make sure that I spend quality time with my loved ones especially my parents and sister. I also believe that God has given me a desire to marry again. I'm trusting God every step of the way. I don't want to make the mistakes that I made before. I'm older, wiser, and more is at stake this time. Like the Bible says, *"When I was a child, I spoke and thought and reasoned as a child. But when I grew up, I put away childish things"* (1 Corinthians 13:11 ESV). I pray that God will continue to show me with distinct clarity, exactly what I'm supposed to do.

I am also learning that a lot of our disappointments, hurts, and aggravations come from when we put people in place of where God should be. My sisters and brothers, we serve a jealous God. His word says, *"You are to have no other gods besides me"* (Exodus 20:3 NET). His word also says, *"Trust in the Lord with all thine heart; and lean not unto thine own understanding. In all thy ways acknowledge Him, and He shall direct thy paths"* (Proverbs 3:6). When we put others before God that is when our disappointment comes.

I'm about to keep it very real with you all. As I mentioned earlier, I went through a divorce that I thought was going to take me out of this world. One of the hardest things I had to balance and learn in life was keeping the peace in this situation because my son's precious life was at stake. One of the hardest things is loving someone you know is not right for you and then letting that person go.

Grow Everyday

One of the signs of resiliency is growth. Growth in certain areas will be evident whereas before there was struggle. I think back on my own life in this book, and you can see I talk about my own experiences. I sometimes wonder about the things we stress about in life and wonder if we really need to stress over them at all. I am starting to learn that if it is not going to matter in 5 years, or even on my death bed, why should I make it matter now? What I'm trying to say is, sometimes we make mountains out of molehills. We need to learn how to compartmentalize things and know which things count, and which things do not. Another part of being resilient, is knowing that these situations will arise but not allowing these situations to break you.

In my previous marriage, the pain that caused us to break up was the fact that my ex-husband had a child I did not know about. I found out about this child after we were married. For the longest time, I was so angry, I mean, I was filled with seething anger. I was so angry towards him for obvious reasons, but I was also so angry towards the child who had nothing to do with any of this. The pain started to lessen when I finally realized that I was growing. A lot of times things happen to us in life and people will say, "Okay that happened, now get over it." Sometimes it's just not that easy to get over. Many times, that moving forward and growth takes years. It was not until almost 7 years later that I started to adjust. I even began to think about having my son spend time with his brother. Granted before this, when Matthew was around 2 years old, he began a relationship with his brother. My ex-husband would have the two of them spend time together when I was not present. To be honest, I wasn't ready and did not want any part of it. Eventually, I started to look at the bigger picture. You may ask, what is the bigger picture? The bigger picture is, no matter what I did or said, I couldn't change one fact: this little boy *is* Matthew's brother. My anger, my feelings, or whatever else I was dealing with, would not change that one immutable fact. I had to realize this is his brother and he should have a relationship with him. No matter what I tried to do, retaliate or hold Matthew back from him, it wouldn't change anything. Point blank, Matthew has a brother who is not my child.

For that relationship to flourish and not be tainted, I had to move past what I felt. I realized that I had grown because before I wasn't even considering the idea of Matthew ever knowing him. I knew I was growing because now I even envisioned Matthew being close with his brother. I have sense in that being resilient, areas that were once painful for you or caused you such pain, you move on from it. You will see and feel a shift in your life. Your emotional indicator will show that to you. The Bible calls us to forgive and not harbor feelings against other people (Matthew 18:15). Only then, will we move forward and become resilient.

Keys to Remember

- We all face troubles
- You can overcome any challenge

- Resilient people encounter challenges but they endure
- Be present every day; enjoy life
- God can take ordinary moments and make them extraordinary
- Trust God's timing, don't try to rush ahead
- God has a divine plan for you
- Stay focused on the things God wants you to do
- As you become resilient, situations will "bounce off" you
- Becoming resilient allows you to move forward from life's challenges

Chapter 3

NURTURE YOURSELF

"Dear friend, I hope all is well with you and that you are as healthy in body as you are strong in spirit" (3 John 1:2 NLT).

In the noise and "clutter" of life, sometimes you must be still. We live in a world where there are so many things vying for our attention, and some of it's not good. These are only distractions. To fully live out the call of God on your life, it is going to take some definite focus and persistence. This is the reason it is so important to make time for you. There is an adage which states, "You are not good for anyone else, if you are not good to yourself". How can we truly help others if we are feeling defeated and depleted?

One of the biggest things I need for you to realize is that we all face challenges. No one is exempt from challenges. We see proof of those who we think have it all, and then later we find out are facing significant issues. Once you come to the realization that you are truly not alone, it may help to lighten the load a little. One thing I know for sure is that you cannot get anything big out of life without getting in the presence of God. Having a relationship with God and walking with Him daily needs to be top priority in your life. You cannot get through this life, without the help of God; however, with God's help, you can do all things. In fact, His word says, *"I can do all things through Christ who strengthens me" (Philippians 4:13 NKJV).* In certain Christian circles, it's taught to give, give, and give, in all ways, but how can you be of any great use when you do not have any energy left. Even Jesus, at times, walked away from the crowd and took time for Himself. He used this time to pray and fellowship with God alone. We see evidence of this in Luke 5:16 (NIV), *"But Jesus often withdrew to lonely places and prayed".*

If the Savior of the world took time for Himself, to pray and be alone, why not us? As believers and ambassadors of Christ, we are to follow and live out His example.

Here is a harsh reality: One day you are going to die. So, while you're here you might as well live. A friend of mine once said, "While alive, live". Please understand, your life is your responsibility. No one is going to save you, and no human can. Only Jesus can save you. You need to look to God, as your source and help. I also believe as we do what we can, God will do what we cannot do, and make things happen on our behalf, but for that to happen, you need to act. *Move* your feet. Get up and do something!

Self-Care Is Necessary

Another important aspect of being resilient is knowing how to nurture yourself. In the demands, of life, we all need to stop and pause sometimes. I remember as I was studying to become a New York State Chaplain, one of the things we learned was self-care. Self-care means to take proper care of yourself and treat yourself well. Self-care is necessary to live successfully. Part of self-care is knowing what works best for you and allowing that to happen. For example, one of the things I do daily for self-care is take a shower as soon as I get home from work or being outside. This allows me to get clean of course, but the warm water is soothing and helps me to relax.

It helps to take away the stress of the day. The next morning, I hop back into the shower to wake myself up. I always shower at least twice a day, maybe more in the summer months because it's so hot outside. I know this sounds simple, but it is something that works for me. I also make a point of getting my nails done- manicure and pedicure. Yes, I want my hands and toes to look pretty, but part of going to the nail salon is relaxation therapy. As most of you know, obviously, writing is another way I nurture myself. Also, music is beyond therapeutic for me. This is another part of my self-care. As I stated earlier, being in a state of resiliency allows the ability for us to "bounce back from life's challenges", and this is the reason therefore I believe self-care is essential. When one takes care of self, he or she can forge ahead through everyday life.

Another aspect of self-care is tending to your health. If you're not taking care of your health, how do you expect to "bounce back" from anything? This is the one body we are given. Treat it well. According to the Bible, our bodies are not our own. *"Do you not know that your bodies are temples of the Holy Spirit, who is in you, whom you have received from God?*

You are not your own" (1 Corinthians 6:19). Let me share a short story with you. Allow me to be honest. When it comes to my health, I will go to every doctor-except the dentist. I don't mind visiting my GYN, General Doctor, or Eye Doctor, but the dentist, no way, Jose! In the past, I would totally slack off when it was time for me to go to the dentist. Well, one day I began feeling this pain in my mouth. I knew it was coming from my back tooth on the right side. At first, it was a little uncomfortable but then it became almost unbearable. I thought to myself, uh-oh I better call the dentist. Thankfully, I could get an appointment right away. I get to the dentist and he immediately takes X-rays. The prognosis wasn't good and my tooth had to be extracted. He elaborated and said there was no way to save it. This is the reason behind the pain I had to endure. That bad tooth had to come out. Let me back up for a minute, you see months before that, I had a root canal and never went back to complete the job. I tried to half-step it; weasel my way out of going back. C'mon, it's the dentist, and who wants to go there? Well, had I not slacked off and had the work completed, I would not have suffered in pain or lost my tooth. This was totally something that could have been prevented. I had to go through because I did not do what I was supposed to do in a certain timeframe. When we do not administer self-care, minor problems that are happening can become major problems. One lesson I learned for sure from all of that is, I will never delay going to the dentist again. In fact, I plan on going every 6 months to maintain my teeth in their healthy condition.

As we nurture ourselves, I believe we become the best versions of us, fit for the Master's use. We need to care for ourselves spiritually and physically. In 3 John 1:2 (NIV), it says, *"Dear friend, I pray that you may enjoy good health and that all may go well with you, even as your soul is getting along well".* Self-care is doing what you need to do for you, to maintain your most optimal health-physically and spiritually.

For self-care maintenance, sometimes you must "unplug" from the world. Sometimes, disconnection from social media is necessary. We live in an age where everything is technology based. While I do believe that technology is a blessing, it can also be a hindrance. Social media has people caught up and trying to live other people's lives that may not be real but appear real on the world wide web. For example, you may have people portraying that they're wealthy, but they are actually broke…but anyway, that's a sidebar, lol. By "unplugging" you alleviate distractions, become quiet, and hear from God. Personally at least once a week, I try to not get on social media, even if it's for a few hours. This helps me clear my mind, hear from God, and work on my goals without distractions. As I said technology is a blessing but I believe there needs to be a balance. Also, by unplugging, you can focus on your greatest project…you.

By nurturing ourselves, we become the best version of us. I also believe that there are still things we must learn about ourselves. When we administer self-care, we can learn or relearn who we truly are. We learn more about our strengths as well as our weaknesses. Whatever is weak in you, you may allow God to purge it from you to help strengthen you. We all have room to grow as we are a work in progress but with God's help, we can move forward into everything that is for us.

Establish Goals

If you do not have a vision for your life, how can you know where you're headed? A part of nurturing ourselves is knowing what we want out of life. Please understand it is okay, you don't have to have all the answers. In fact, none of us do. This is the reason we have to rely on God to show us.

I want you to take a minute and think about what you want to accomplish during your lifetime. When your eulogy is read at your funeral, what do you want it to say? None of us are going to exist in this physical body forever. So, while you are here, as Diddy would say, "Get it done!" There is no time for games. Your legacy depends on it. And, especially if you have children, they are counting on you. I will give you a few ideas. If you've always wanted to go back to school, enroll. If you always wanted to write a book, start writing. If you've been thinking about starting a business, do it. If you always wanted to travel, go! Whatever is in your mind to do, and it's legal, and doesn't affect your relationship with God, I say **do it!** Time waits for no woman, man, or child. While you are here, I encourage you to go after the things God has placed in your heart. And, no, you are

not too old. God has a great work for you to do, my friend. Although there is an abundance of opportunities around you, there is not an abundance of time. Steve Jobs, a famous entrepreneur who co-founded Apple Inc., once said, "Your time is limited, so don't waste it living someone else's life. Don't be trapped by dogma – which is living with the results of other's thinking. Don't let the noise of other's opinions drown out your own inner voice, and most important, have the courage to follow your heart and intuition. They somehow already know what you truly want to become. Everything else is secondary."

One of my goals was to write a book. And, thankfully by God's grace, I did that. This one you're reading is my second. To God be the glory! Alleluia! God is truly awesome! I also want to encourage you to continue to work on your goals, don't be concerned that you are behind time. While you're taking action, just know that everything will fall into place at God's time. The main thing is that you have establish goals, and now you're taking action to fulfill them.

"This vision is for a future time. It describes the end, and it will be fulfilled. If it seems slow in coming, wait patiently, for it will surely take place. It will not be delayed (Habakkuk 2:3 NLT)." I also believe when we establish goals, it allows us to know that we have purpose. Some people feel that their life is meaningless, and I believe it is because they feel purposeless. When you have goals that you are working toward, you tend to keep your "eyes on the prize". It's like a runner during a marathon. That person's goal is to get to the finish line. Even as harsh as the trail may be, they keep running because they have a goal in mind. This is where they keep their focus. You have to *set your face like a flint (Isaiah 50:7)*, and keep working towards your goals.

Celebrate Your Uniqueness

There was a time in my life when I did not appreciate my uniqueness. I actually felt bad that I did not think like everybody else. I would often wonder to myself in my 20s why things like parties and hanging out did not really interest me. Although, I would go out with my friends from time to time. My peers on the other hand, would engage often in such things. I really felt as if something was wrong with me. I would think to myself why am I this way, and why am I not like everybody else? Why don't I want to party, why don't I want to hang out, or just seem to live life frivolously? Then, I realized that God created me for a difference.

In His word, God chooses whom He loves, and He often calls the unqualified and the overlooked (1 Corinthians 1:27-29). What man discredits, God gives credit. Often, the people who are discarded, God chooses to use for His own divine purpose. Now the older I get, the more I appreciate my difference. You see, my beloved believers, God has set you aside for His own purpose. God wants us to be consecrated and set apart. Sanctification means separation. The word says for us to come apart, to be set apart, to be made for the Maker's use. Now, I'm thankful I'm not like the others. I am thankful that the things that are interesting and engaging to this world, are not much interest to me. When God calls you, He is going to choose you for His own purpose. He is going to download things into your spirit that are unlike anything else. For example, things that may have interest you before, may no longer interest you

now. Places that you would go to before, you would no longer go to now. When you really start to walk with God, and live out your purpose, you will start to think how God thinks. Remember, in His word, He says, *"As the heavens are higher than the earth, so are my ways higher than your ways and my thoughts than your thoughts" (Isaiah 55:9 NLT).*
. The Bible also instructs us to think on certain things. Therefore, when you think on things that are of God, it will be different than the way the world thinks.

Be thankful for your uniqueness. It is your uniqueness that will set you apart. People who have done great things in life, are set apart. If you look at the world's greatest inventors, authors, athletes, physicians etc., they are people who have chosen to run their own race. They *chose.* They made a cognizant decision to not follow the crowd. People who have won a Nobel Peace Prize, or Nobel laureates, are people who have chosen to do things their own way. When God chooses you, He's not choosing you so that you can do things in the way the world does. Look at our Savior Jesus Christ. He was a man who was chosen by God and decided to follow God all the way. During His time, He was considered a rebel, a revolutionary. Think about that word revolutionary. Often, a revolution is started by people who are not satisfied with the status quo and basically sick, tired and fed up with things in the present. If you want to make a distinctive change, you need to be revolutionary in your thinking and how you move according to God's word. People who have made the greatest change are often those who have taken the greatest stance. There is a common saying, "If you don't stand for something, you will fall for anything." Pray on it, seek God with **every** area of your life, and He will direct you on what to do. Trust the Holy Spirit's leading, in what He would have you to do. The word says, "*In all thy ways acknowledge Him, and He shall direct your paths" (Proverbs 3:6)*. When you acknowledge God in every area of your life, He will give you clarity, understanding, and wisdom. The Bible says that "*Wisdom is the principal thing; therefore, get wisdom: and with all thy getting get understanding" (Proverbs 4:7)*. I have learned, that sometimes you must tune out the voices of people. People are not walking in your shoes. They are not walking your path, and they are not fulfilling your destiny. Your destiny is chosen by God. Now, His

Word says, "*Thou shalt also decree a thing, and it shall be established unto thee: and the light shall shine upon thy ways" (Job 22:28).* So, whatever is on your heart to fulfill, whatever is your life passion, pursue it. You will discover your purpose when you discover and celebrate your uniqueness. Your uniqueness is a clue to your assignment on this earth. As you've heard me say before, God gives us different assignments and different purposes that we are to fulfill. Your assignment is great. Don't let anyone tell you that your assignment is insignificant or unimportant. Take time out today to purposefully seek out God in prayer, and if need be, fasting. As, you trust God, I truly believe that He will unveil everything that you need to know, to fulfill your unique purpose. Be blessed and always forge ahead, knowing that God wants you to succeed.

Declutter Your Mind

Often, people will have an opinion about your life. But, they fail to realize that they are not walking in your shoes. As people of God, we must be attuned to the Holy Spirit. The Word says, *"But when He, the*

Spirit of truth, comes, He will guide you into all the truth. He will not speak on his own; He will speak only what He hears, and He will tell you what is yet to come" (John 16:13 NIV). For every problem you may face, the Bible has the answer.

We must make time to spend in God's presence. Remember, God created you and knows everything about you. As you trust in God, He will renew your strength. Find time each day to get with God in a quiet space. Take time to pray and time to read His word. As you sit quietly before God, He will download ideas and answers to the problems you may face.

I recall in my own life when I was given advice that I needed to be busier. However, as I listened to that advice, something was unsettled in my spirit. In other words, it didn't resonate with my spirit. It didn't seem like it fit me. It also didn't seem like the best thing at the time, but when I sat quietly before God and prayed, He gave me different advice. He gave me specific instructions: I needed to be selective and strategic. So, the advice I received from a human, was contrary to what God deposited in my spirit. Often what the world says to do, will be contrary to God's instructions, but as people of God, we should realize that God does not operate in a "cookie-cutter" fashion. He has uniquely created each one of us in His own design. We are different. The fact that no two humans on this earth are alike is brilliant!

The world will have you believe that believing in God is out of style. The world will try to entice you with things that seem spectacular and things of the flesh. His Word will give you life. *"For they are life to those who find them, and healing to all their flesh" (Proverbs 4:22 ESV).*

I cannot impress it upon you enough to study and read God's word. His word has the answer to every problem, obstacle, and challenge you may ever face in your lifetime. He loves you with an everlasting love (Jeremiah 31:3).

Everyone is not going to celebrate what God is doing in your life. This is why you have to push forward in spite of the obstacles and naysayers. *"And let us not be weary in well doing: for in due season we shall reap, if we faint not" (Galatians 6:9).* As humans, we all want a cheerleading squad. At times, we are looking for others to encourage and inspire us. However, sometimes like David, we have to encourage ourselves in the Lord. Sometimes, your team may be made up of two people, you and God. *"With God, all things are possible"* (Luke 1:37). You cannot fail and you will succeed. Trust God with everything and the timing of your life.

Like a horse that has blinders on, set your face like a flint and move forward. When you are pursuing your God-given purpose, you don't have time for any distractions. Please know this right now and right here, everyone is not going to be on the sidelines rooting for you as you pursue your purpose. There will be people who will actually be upset with you because you decided to do something greater than yourself.

At the end of our lives, I believe God will ask us what have we done with the gifts that He gave us. At that point, you do not want to come up short. At that point, it's not going to matter who was for you, or who was against you. At that point, you cannot say, "Oh, I'm sorry Lord I decided not to fulfill my God-given purpose because I was more concerned about what people had to say." The awesomeness of God is that He does not consult with people when He appoints and designs our purpose.

People will say it is not black-and-white. But, I beg to differ when it comes to God. God is very clear on what He requires of His people. Just read His Word, if you don't believe me. God wants people to be set free, delivered, and flowing in the fullness of their purpose. God wants people to come into the knowledge of Jesus Christ. God wants people saved from the depths of hell and to have new life in Him.

Many Gifts, Many Activities

There's a common understanding, or misunderstanding, rather, that one should stay on one career path. People tend to forget that we are created in the image of God. Realize that God created the earth in seven days. The earth with all of its' magnificence and glory, cannot compare to the awesomeness of God. Therefore, since we are created in the image of God, we can do all things, and His word says so. I truly believe that God gives us various gifts and talents, but it is up to us if we use them. Remember, this is the one life you have been given. Use it to its fullest, and give it all you've got! I remember when God led me to become a chaplain. At the present time, I was also teaching. I remember sharing it with a teacher colleague of mine. And, her response was, "Are you going to leave teaching to do that?" And I told her, "No, I plan to do it in tandem." By her expression, I can tell she could not fathom how I could possibly do both. But, when you are in Christ His word says that we can do all things. It is by the spirit of God that we are empowered to move forward in our gifts and do all and be all that God has created us to be.

Becoming resilient and exercising resilience, you need to use your gifts and various resources to move ahead. That means delving deep into oneself and discovering the many gifts and talents that are embedded in you. The Holy Spirit drops ideas, visions, and goals for you to pursue, but God does not force His will on us. It is up to us to move with decisive action into the things that He is calling us to do. When you're resilient, there is a transformation that takes place. You begin to see things with a new set of eyes and a new vision takes up residence in your heart.

Don't Complain, Construct Ideas

The caption says it all, but let me elaborate as I give an example. In relationships, we may expect others to meet our needs. We must realize though, that God is the only one who can meet all of our needs. I recall a particular time in my life where I kept making a repeated request. It appeared as though I was nagging and being overly persistent. When in my opinion, I was only trying to get my point across. I kept stating, "I need this and I need that, etc." I kept repeating myself to no avail. I then realized to not complain about things unless I was willing to change them. You see the only person who can create effective change in your life is you. As the saying goes, you are the master of your destiny. We cannot expect mere humans to give us all we need. When we do this, this creates an atmosphere of confusion and disappointment. We may also tend to feel resentful and regretful. You are one decision away from changing the course of your life. Remember, only you can create the lasting change you seek.

Think about the things that bring you fulfillment. Dwell on the things that bring you peace and joy. What makes you happy? What are some of your interests? What makes you want to get out of bed in the morning with zeal and purpose? What do you want your legacy to be?

This is about constructing and devising a plan to fulfill your purpose. There is no use in complaining, because sometimes people are not listening. Take an inventory of the things that interest you. Make a list of ten things that bring you the most joy. Try to incorporate those activities into your day. Even if you cannot do all ten, try to incorporate several of them. For example, I enjoy reading and writing. I incorporate this daily into my life. For me to have peace of mind, I need to read and write. It's therapeutic for me. In addition, music is also my solace. I enjoy and love playing my flute. Even when I am not creating melodies, I still enjoy practicing. The tone and the sound of the flute brings me a sense of peace. Since every one of us are different, our interests will be varied. Begin to *learn* and *love you*. You may even have to find time to separate yourself from people. Make time for you in whatever capacity that may be. Unbeknownst to them, people can drain you. Even those that you love, will drain you. You, along with the help of God, can truly take care of you.

Find Your Voice

This day and age, where there are so many counterfeit and copycats, be true to yourself. The world will have you believe that you are inadequate, if you don't rise and go with the flow of today's trend. I truly believe there are more women today who are insecure with themselves and unsatisfied with who God created them to be. The world will have you to believe that you need to be a certain cup size, or a certain hip size, to have any value. *"I praise you because I am fearfully and wonderfully made; your works are wonderful; I know that full well" (Psalm 139:14).* God has made you unique. There is no one like you on this earth. Be thankful that God created you in His own design.

I recall a time in my own life when I felt inadequate. Because of the betrayal I suffered in my marriage, I felt as if I was not "pretty enough", and so many negative thoughts flooded my head. During my journey to resilience, I have learned this: just because someone does not see your value, it does not mean you are worthless. Find your value in God. While becoming resilient, I have learned to never make anyone your idol. The only one who should be worshipped and adored is God. God is who we should chase and give first place in our lives. Only God can truly satisfy.

Keys to Remember

- Get in to God's presence daily
- Your relationship with God needs to be top priority
- Take time for yourself to avoid burnout
- Nurturing yourself will allow you to become the best version of yourself
- Establish goals for your life
- Celebrate your uniqueness
- You are an original, not a photocopy
- Declutter your mind by unplugging from social media periodically
- Put your gifts to use
- Ideas will flow when you are still
- Be who God created you to be

Chapter 4

SERVE OTHERS

"For even the Son of Man came not to be served but to serve others and to give his life as a ransom for many" (Matthew 20:28 NLT).

I am a firm believer that God will use everything that has happened to us for growth and guide us to our destiny. One of my favorite pastors, Joyce Meyer said, "Get busy being a blessing to someone; do something fruitful." I totally agree with this. While God is busy working out our problems, we should go and be a blessing to someone else.

Our lives are not our own. We were bought with a price (1 Corinthians 6:20). I believe one of the most fulfilling things in life is when you can help someone else. Sometimes, when we get the focus off us, we realize that the problems we are facing are not so bad.

My job as a New York State Chaplain requires me to serve others. I remember one day I was feeling bad and had to go pay a visit to the nursing home.

The minute I walked in, I felt the love and appreciation from the staff and other patients. As I sat with my patient who has Alzheimer's, I realized the things that were concerning me were not so bad. I began to be thankful for my health and the many blessings I did have. Serving others helps us to get the focus off our problems. It helps us to look at the bigger picture. When we serve others, we honor God. Even when no one else sees us serving, God sees. Remember, nothing is hidden from His sight. I believe God sees our good works, and it glorifies Him. Matthew 5:16 says, *"In the same way, let your light shine before others, that they may see your good deeds and glorify your Father in heaven."* This clearly shows that when people see our good deeds, they will know that there is a God, and glorify Him. I truly believe when we serve others, it enables them to see God at work in us.

Having a servant's heart is being an example of Jesus. In Acts 10:38 it says, *"How God anointed Jesus of Nazareth with the Holy Ghost and with power: who went about doing good, and healing all that were oppressed of the devil; for God was with Him."*

Serving others is another way to give back. I also believe as we serve others, it encourages other people to do the same and it causes a "ripple effect". I also believe serving others is another way to show our gratitude. And, gratitude opens the door for more blessings to enter our lives.

Serving others, serves others. It really does! It helps the person you are serving to know that they are loved, appreciated, and cared for. This is especially true if they are non-believers as it may open them to want to know more about our Savior Jesus. And, yes serving others may include sharing the gospel. But, it may also be in sharing ordinary things, such as cooking for someone, doing their grocery shopping, helping with laundry, etc. There are so many ways that we can help other people around us.

We can learn a lot about service through the life of Ruth. Ruth was the daughter-in-law of Naomi. When Ruth's husband died, she told Naomi she will not leave her. "*Don't urge me to leave you or turn back from you. Where you go I will go, and where you stay I will stay. Your people will be my people and your God my God (Ruth 1:16 NIV).*" Ruth continued to stay faithful to Naomi and stayed by serving in the fields. As the story continues, Ruth ends up receiving a great blessing by meeting Boaz. During that time, he was the wealthiest man on the land. He noticed Ruth's loyalty, dedication, and hard work and was very impressed. Long story short, Boaz and Ruth married. As you see, one of your greatest blessings will come by serving other people.

Another great biblical example of service, is the life of Joshua. Before Joshua became a leader, he was a humble servant and loyal follower of Moses. We learn from watching the life of Joseph that a good leader serves other people. A life of service prepares you for leadership. Because of his loyalty and servanthood towards Moses, Joshua is commissioned to take over as leader. Joshua was on an assignment to serve Moses from God. "*If you are faithful in little things, you will be faithful in large ones. But if you are dishonest in little things, you won't be honest with greater responsibilities (Luke 16:10 NIV).*"

As a New York State chaplain, and the founder of Be An Overcomer, Inc. I am called to serve people. I was having a conversation with a friend, and I shared with her how I know God has called me to outreach ministry. I am not saying that I will not stand at a pulpit and preach, however, I know for sure God is calling me to be out there amongst the people. If you look at the life of Jesus, you will see that a majority of His ministry was outreach. In Luke 14:23, it reads, "*And the lord said unto the servant, Go out into the highways and hedges, and compel them to come in, that my house may be filled.*"

Serving Others Glorifies God

Serving others glorifies God for non-believers. As many people as we may want to serve, we cannot serve everyone. But, those that we do serve will benefit from it. A majority of Jesus' ministry was service. He taught us that we are to serve others, care for people, and love them. "*By this everyone will know that you are my disciples, if you love one another (John 13:35 NIV).*" People will take notice when we serve others. They may reject God, but it's hard to reject or deny Him, when you see God at work in someone's life.

Serving Increases Our Faith

Serving helps to encourage you. I truly believe when we encourage other people, we help to encourage ourselves. When we serve others by encouragement, it serves as a reminder to us as well. As you speak those faith-filled words, you give life to your spirit. Every morning, I post on my social media an encouraging word as part of my, Be An Overcomer ministry. Many times, the feedback I get is amazing! People will often tell me how my word was right on time, or that it was something they needed to hear. Not realizing, the word that I give is also encouraging me but also reminding myself of God's goodness. The Bible speaks of how David encouraged himself in the Lord (1 Samuel 30:6). As believers, we know that words give life and have power. It is so important to speak faith-filled, edifying words.

Serving Demonstrates God's Love

As we serve others through encouragement, we serve and bless ourselves as well. Also, as you serve others through encouragement, you somehow by God's grace contribute to their growth. Serving others helps to inspire people you know, and many that you may never meet. A life of service is admirable. As believers, we should be compelled to help others. This will help to edify and strengthen their spiritual walk. For those that are non-believers it will pique their interest to know the One and true living God.

Several years ago, in the movie *Pay It Forward,* the character Trevor starts an experiment about doing good deeds. His one good deed, led to another person doing a good deed, and so forth and so on. The result caused a ripple effect of a whole community helping and serving one another. I believe this is the reason serving others is so important. As we serve others, we begin to demonstrate the love of God. According to John 13:35, when we love one another through service, we show that we belong to God.

Keys to Remember

- As believers, we are called to serve others
- Serving others helps to get the focus off us
- When we serve others, we honor God
- Serving is a way to give back

- Serving others is demonstrating God's love
- When we serve, it causes a ripple effect
- Serving glorifies God before non-believers
- Serving is a way to encourage yourself
- When we serve, we show that we are God's people
- Serving helps us to be like Jesus
- Serving opens our heart to joy
- By serving others, our faith is increased
- Serve where you are planted
- Look for opportunities to serve
- A good leader serves other people
- Serving other people prepares you for leadership
- When we serve, it allows us to experience God's presence

Chapter 5

WALK IN FAITH

"For we walk by faith, not by sight"
(2 Corinthians 5:7).

Several years ago, I was going through so much turmoil in my life. My marriage was falling apart. My friend, Cherise Irons, invited me to a bible study. Little did I know then that my life was about to dramatically change. The minister, Vivian Allen, was leading the bible study that night, and I remember Cherise telling me that Vivian was very prophetic and had a deep understanding about the word of God. Little did I know that Vivian would be instrumental in my restoration process. As long as I live, I will never forget the first few words she said to me. "Women of God, don't you know that the breaking of you, is the making of you?"

The "breaking of me" was me releasing and almost forgetting all that I knew, and pressing forward into the new season that God had for me. Back in 2010, all I knew was being a wife, mother, daughter, and a friend. And, yes of course, I was a musician. But, I wasn't creating and composing my own music. As my world was shaken by the divorce, I began to question what was next for me. I felt as if my ex-husband was my world. A great part of my life was focused and centered on him. And, when he disappointed me through betrayal, I did not know what to do. I started to question everything. Even my own existence. I did not feel worthy or feel like living.

Put God First

It is a dangerous thing when you make someone an idol. Worshipping someone else other than God is something the Bible warns against. *"You shall have no other gods before me"* (Exodus 20:3 NIV). We serve a jealous God, and our faith has to solely rest in Him. Not people. People are fallible, and they will frustrate and fail you at times.

Stay in Faith

"For we walk by faith, not by sight" (2Corinthians 5:7), Or, as my friend, Chini Carney says, "We walk by faith, and not by our feelings." I often find that what we are believing for is contrary to

what we see in the natural. For example, you may be believing for financial freedom, while being overwhelmed in debt. You may have received a negative doctor's report, but believing for restoration of your health. I have learned and continue to learn to not allow what you see in the natural to deter what your spirit believes.

Look Beyond What You See in the Natural

Sometimes, as humans we are scared to walk in faith, because of fear of the unknown. We may have deep rooted hindering beliefs as to why we are not walking in faith. It is important to examine and look beyond the surface of why we fear walking in faith. As my friend, Chini Carney, says, "We have to force and pull those roots out." "*Therefore, since we are surrounded by such a huge crowd of witnesses to the life of faith, let us strip off every weight that slows us down, especially the sin that so easily trips us up. And let us run with endurance the race God has set before us*" (Hebrews 12:1 NLT). As believers, we must remember fear is not of God. "*For God hath not given us the spirit of fear; but of power, and of love, and of a sound mind* (2 Timothy 1:7)." A renown pastor, Christine Caine, once said, "Build your life on the truth of the Word of God, and not on the facts of your circumstances." I am learning daily that we are to walk by faith, and allow our faith to change our circumstances.

Trust God Through the Process

Here is a question for you. Can you trust God through the process? Things that are designed to break you down, will build you up. Things that are designed to tear you apart, will take you up. This is the reason why we as believers must demonstrate faith in God and His Word. "*And we know that in all things God works for the good of those who love him, who have been called according to his purpose*" (Romans 8:28 NIV). Sometimes things happen in life that we may not understand. I believe that God will use everything that has happened to us for our greater good. All of this "stuff" that we go through good or bad, is to work out a greater purpose in us, and we must trust God through it as we walk by faith.

Faith Over Fear

Walking in faith also means that you fear God and trust Him more than you do man. Remember, man is finite in his wisdom, but God's wisdom is infinite. God sees around the hidden corners and details that we may have no clue about. God is aware of every second of our lives! When we walk by faith, we choose to trust God in every circumstance over our own thinking. The Bible speaks of how God rewards those who diligently seek Him (Hebrews 11:6). And how do we seek God, you might ask? We do this by walking in faith. I believe when we choose to go against our natural desires and walk in faith, we will see God's power manifest in our lives. I also believe that in order to see our full potential and realize the call of God on our life, we have to walk by faith. As a believer, the very core of why we believe in God, is because we have faith in Him. *"I am the Alpha and the Omega--the beginning and the end," says the Lord God. "I am the one who is, who always was, and who is still to come--the Almighty One" (Revelation 1:8 NLT).*

I want to share another story with you. As I was going through my divorce, God told me that this period would be a time of transition. Transition means change. No one likes or wants to change. We are creatures of habit and do things a certain way. Once we are comfortable doing things a certain way, it can be hard to break out of that mold. Usually God will give me a word for the various seasons of life. During that time, I heard distinctly the word, transition. In 2015, I went through so many changes; even down to my hair, lol. At that time, God told me to stop relaxing my hair and transition from permed to natural hair. Several changes took place. I moved from one town to another on Long Island. That was a change. I went from being a married woman to a single woman. That was a change. I began to let go of certain habits that were holding me back and began to eat healthier. That was a change. God also said that my son Matthew would be incorporated into that transition period. He went from Pre-school to all day Kindergarten, in a new school; new town. That was a complete change. I shared this story with you so that you can see the changes I went through. I believe the key element that got me through that time was my faith. In order to go through that season, I had to trust God and walk in faith. If I did not operate in faith, I believe I would have had a meltdown. In the natural, the challenges I faced seemed insurmountable but with God's help and walking in faith, I got through it.

Walking on Water

Imagine you going all out for God. Imagine that you push past the noise of this life and go full-fledge into everything that God is calling you to do. Yes, it's challenging. Yes, it's not going to be easy, but the rewards far outweigh the challenges. God is calling us to higher and deeper in Him. We are not called to lead mundane and ordinary lives. We serve an extraordinary God. Therefore, He wants to do exceedingly great things in and through us.

Like Peter, we need to step out of the boat and relinquish our fears and walk on the water towards Jesus. Pay no attention to the naysayers, the haters, the negative talkers in your ear. Only heed and listen to the voice of God. In Jeremiah 1:5, God speaks of how He knew us before He formed us in our mother's womb. There is a great work for you to do. And, through God you can do it all.

How to Walk in Faith

Here are a few ways to walk by faith. The first step is to know that you need God. Without Him, you can't do anything. He is the very source of your life, and the reason you are still here on earth.

"I am the vine; you are the branches. If you remain in me and I in you, you will bear much fruit; apart from me you can do nothing" (John 15:5 NIV). The second is to recognize that God is your savior and ask for His direction. As Jeremiah 29:11 reminds us, God has a good plan for our lives. God knows exactly what you need and the timing of it. He knows how to get you through the storms of life. *"In all your ways acknowledge Him, And He will make your paths straight" (Proverbs 3:6 NASB).* God will help you and guide you. The third step is to research and find scriptures pertaining to your situation. For example, if you need healing, find healing scriptures. If you're in a financial crisis, find scriptures pertaining to finances. There is an answer to every problem you will ever face. And, it is found in the Word of God. As you begin to meditate on the Word of God, allow it to saturate into your spirit. Let it take deep root within you. Speak God's word daily over your life and the

situations you face. It's not enough to just read His Word; you need to speak His Word as well. The fourth step is to act upon everything aforementioned. We will not see our faith at work until we work our faith. *"In the same way, faith by itself, if it is not accompanied by action, is dead" (James 2:17 NIV).* As we see, it is not enough to say we have faith. We must demonstrate and act on our faith. I truly believe then, and only then, will we see God's promises manifested in our lives. So, today, I encourage you to take action on the things you are believing God for and watch Him move on your behalf in His timing.

Keys to Remember

- The breaking of you, is the making of you
- Keep God first
- Seek Him in prayer daily
- Don't allow your feelings to deter what your spirit believes
- Look beyond the natural realm
- As you walk in faith, God will reveal His purpose for you

- As you walk in faith, trust God through the process
- Walking in faith means you trust God more over man's opinion
- Walking in faith allows us to see God's power at work in our lives
- By walking in faith, we choose to trust God in every circumstance
- When we walk in faith, we see God's promises manifested in our lives

Chapter 6

FORGET THE PAST

'Remember not the former things, nor consider the things of old. Behold, I am doing a new thing; now it springs forth, do you not perceive it? I will make a way in the wilderness and rivers in the desert"
(Isaiah 43:18-19 ESV).

By now, you all know that I suffered great pain in my former marriage. I also know at one point in time, I had great love for him. At first, I constantly blamed him for the issues in our marriage. I felt that if he would stop running around, cheating, and remain faithful, that everything would be better, but as the saying goes, "Hurt people, hurt people." After seeking God in much needed prayer and meditation, things began to be revealed to me.

One day my ex-husband asked me to proofread a paper he wrote for a class. In the paper, he described in great detail the issues his family had faced. Through reading this paper, the Holy Spirit revealed to me that the philandering issues with women and partying started with his grandfather. The Holy Spirit also revealed that it was a generational curse that had been passed down. I also remember going to a prayer service, and the bishop of that church prophesied and spoke and said that the generational curse stops with my son. He confirmed the word that God already spoke to me previously.

Pray and Fast

As believers, we know that certain strongholds are only broken through prayer and fasting (Matthew 17:21). Another aspect to becoming resilient is forgetting the past. We must move forward into all that God has for us so we can forget past hurt, pain, disappointments, etc. When we dwell on past hurts, it allows for it to be embedded in our hearts and minds. It can take years, maybe a lifetime to recover. Dwelling on past hurts does not hurt the person who has done you wrong, it hurts you. You may feel like holding a grudge or wishing bad on the person, but the only person affected by it will be you. Choosing to stay in pain and reliving it daily will take a tremendous toll on you. Meanwhile, your accuser is living free and going about his or her life.

Your Future is Bright

I know it's hard to forget painful situations, but God has more for you to think about. Your future will be better than your past. You must believe that. As a believer, you have a covenant right for this to be so.

Emotional stability comes from being able to let things go. The more you hold onto pain, the more you hinder your progress in the process of moving forward. Forgetting the past is to move forward in faith, knowing that what is coming is better than what has been. I have come to realize that pain is a part of your purpose, and purpose will push you to your promise. This means that whatever we desire, or whatever the will of God is for us, it will require stretching on our part.

Birth Your Promise

I am reminded about the time I had to deliver my son, Matthew. For those of us women who have experienced natural childbirth, you know that it is a painful process. Yet the promise of having your precious little baby in your arms far outweighs the pain of delivery. While in the delivery room, your obstetrician is going to encourage you to "push past the pain." Once you do that, your "promise", your baby, will be delivered.

Please understand, no one is exempt from pain. As long as you are here on this earth, you are going to experience some sort of pain. The amazing thing about God is that He is with us every step of the way. His Word even states, we are *"more than conquerors"* (Romans 8:37). This means we can overcome anything! Be encouraged by this. There is something greater for you when you choose to forget the past, and press toward your future. Keep pressing and fight the good fight of faith!

Take Responsibility for your Life

There is a common saying that God is in control. I believe, though, that people use this as an excuse, to not except responsibility for themselves. When people say God is in control, it's as if they are saying whatever will be, will be. People fail to realize, that in the beginning, God gave us dominion and authority. He has also given us the gift of free will. In His word, it says *"Death and life are in the power of the tongue"*

(Proverbs 18:21). He also says that we can "Decree a thing and it shall be established" (Job 22:28). In Romans 4:17 NIV, it says, "*God who gives life to the dead and calls into being things that were not.*" So, therefore, God has given us a choice about the matters and situations in our lives. While I do believe at times, God's sovereignty overrides everything; however, I also believe that we can speak and declare things into our lives and they will come to pass. While you're waiting on God, God is waiting on you. While you're saying God is in control, God is waiting to see what you are going to say and do about your situation. I truly believe God rewards those that help themselves. For example, while you do what you can, God will do what you cannot do. But I don't think people should expect to sit and do absolutely nothing and yet expect God to do the miraculous in their life.

Commit to Excellence

God wants us to do everything in excellence. "*But all things should be done decently and in order*" *(1 Corinthians 14:40 ESV).* Become a person who is committed to excellence. I truly believe that when we do things in an excellent manner, God rewards us.

What I'm trying to say: don't take shortcuts. As I reflect upon this, I recall a time I went to the grocery store. After leaving the store, I unloaded my cart, put my groceries in the car, and proceeded to put the cart back at the cart station. As I walked up to the cart station, I noticed many of the shopping carts were in disarray. Now I understand there is a specific person or worker designated to organize the carts, but as I realize that men may not be able to see our every move, however, God does. *"The eyes of the LORD search the whole earth in order to strengthen those whose hearts are fully committed to him" (2 Chronicles 16:9 NLT).* God is always watching. God is always looking to see how His servants are operating in His kingdom. As believers, we are to do things in an excellent manner and in an excellent order. We are not to do things haphazardly.

As I walked up to the cart station I noticed that the carts were in disarray and I decided to fix them. Now, I could've walked away like everyone else and went about my day, but I realized that God's watching. I am committed, as a believer, to excellence in and with all things. I needed to not only put my cart back, but I made sure the other few carts that were out of order were organized. *"If you are faithful in little things, you will be faithful in large ones. But if you are dishonest in little things, you won't be honest with greater responsibilities" (Luke 16:10 NLT).*

There are times when we ask God to do great things in our life. We are asking God to take us from the pit to the palace in a matter of days, and some of us expect a turnaround in a matter of hours! We don't realize there are steps that should take place for us to see that promise come to realization. I really believe, that God looks for those whom He can trust. It starts with the little things. Many people may think that my cart organization was miniscule, but God does not believe my work was in vain. So, I urge you to do everything in excellence even when you don't feel like it. This is when it's most especially important. Listen, believers, we can't be led to do the right thing only when it feels right. We are to do things even when it *doesn't* feel right, even when it may seem a challenge, even when we may not fully understand, or even when we may be confused. We are to be committed to excellence and do everything in decency and in order.

When you look at life, you realize that it is limited. Life is a one-way deal. Life is a *limited edition.* You only get one chance to have and live up to your potential. You don't want to waste the opportunity you have been given. Yes, opportunities are limitless. But the time that we have is limited. It's so important to know and discern your purpose from God, and I believe it is done by forgetting the past, pressing forward, and moving in excellence.

You Have Gifts within You

What's in your hand? What are the gifts you have been given? What are some ideas you have that can help you elevate to the next level? If you are not putting it to use, it is no one's fault but your own. Don't blame God for your mishaps. And things that you should be doing. People sometimes don't like to accept responsibility for themselves or the choices they make. At some point, we all have to accept responsibility for our life, and where we are at the present moment. You cannot do anything to change the past, but you can do everything about the future. Change and forgetting the past starts with you. My dear friends, God loves you more than you can ever imagine. Push past the pain and forward into your greatness. Your destiny is too great to sit and stew about the pains of the past. Press forward, Overcomers!

Release the Past

One of the first steps to forgetting the past and moving forward in what God has for you is to acknowledge that you have pain. Another favorite of mine, Paula White says, "You cannot conquer what you will not confront." You must know that you're in pain, and you must let go. You will not know it if you stay in denial believing that you're not hurt.

The next step is to speak about how you feel. Find someone you feel comfortable with and begin to confide in that person. This must be someone you trust to keep matters confidential. If you don't have anyone in your circle, seek out a counselor. That hurt and pain you're feeling, must be released. Be honest with yourself; what the pain did to you, how you reacted to being hurt, etc. Please understand this process most likely will not happen overnight. Be patient with yourself and trust God's process for you. Some people, it may take months in counseling to deal with the pain of their past. You cannot move forward unless you release the past.

The third step is to not declare yourself a victim. Remember, "*We are more than conquerors*" (Romans 8:37)." We are victors not victims! We can be victorious through any situation in life, because we are not alone. God is with us. In adopting a victor's mentality, you must know that you're the captain of your life. You can direct and steer your way to happiness. You cannot rely on others to make you happy. You and God as a team, are a powerful force. There is nothing you cannot overcome and accomplish! This is where some soul-searching takes place as you decide what makes your heart sing. While alive, live! God has purpose for you! You are not a victim! You can do anything through Christ! He gives us strength to achieve and become anything we desire in life. Instead of thinking about what hurt you, announce and affirm the previous declarations for a purpose-filled, victorious life.

Another key to releasing and forgetting the past is to stop replaying the hurt in your head like a broken record. Some people keep replaying the hurt over and over in their heads. This is not good and helpful for your well-being. When you begin to shift your focus, and think about the positive aspects of your life, things will begin to change. The Word speaks about renewing our mind in Romans 12:2. I truly believe the only way we can have a renewed mind, is by seeing things in God's perspective. This can only happen when we renew our mind to His Word. This is the reason why it's so important to get in His Word daily. The life of the believer is a Word-led life. Your thinking should mimic God's thinking.

The last step is to forgive those who've hurt you. As I said earlier in this chapter, holding on to hurt only hurts you. The world may think forgiving others is weak, but forgiving others demonstrates great strength. God knows that it is not easy for us, especially because we're still in this flesh. God encourages us to be led by the Spirit and not our flesh.

I know in my own life; it took a lot for me to forgive my ex-husband, but now I feel so free! It's amazing because the very thing that I thought was going to kill me, made me stronger. Had I not experienced that level of hurt, I do not believe that my ministry, books, and music, would flow through me as they have. It's mind-boggling at times how our pain *really* pushes us to our purpose.

So, today, I encourage you to forget the past hurts and release them to God. Remember, He cares about every detail of your life. He will never lead you astray. Like Paul in the Bible, we need to realize there is a benefit, a reward in moving forward. Everything you desire comes from moving forward in Christ! *"Brothers and sisters, I do not consider myself yet to have taken hold of it. But one thing I do: Forgetting what is behind and straining toward what is ahead" (Philippians 3:13 NIV).*

Keys to Remember

- Your future will be better than your past
- Choose daily to press forward into your future
- We become emotionally stable when we learn to let things go
- Forgetting the past is to move forward in faith
- Pain pushes us to our purpose
- You can overcome anything
- As believers, we have authority over the situations in our lives

- To forget the past, acknowledge the pain first
- Speak about and seek counseling if necessary
- Realize you are a victor and not a victim
- Forget the past by not replaying hurtful situations in your mind
- Think on the positive aspects of your life
- Renew your mind to God's word daily
- Speak life over the situations of your life
- Focus on the goodness of God

Chapter 7
BE GRATEFUL

"Be thankful in all circumstances, for this is God's will for you who belong to Christ Jesus" (1 Thessalonians 5:18 NLT).

My dear Overcomers, we live in such a world where everything is done now and fast. I call it a "microwave-type society." Because we are in such a fast-paced world, we may tend to forget what patience is. I believe this happens because we tend to forget how much progress we have made but continue to focus on how far we must go. Everything happens in *His* timing. God hears your prayers and knows every concern that's on your heart. But while you're in the process of waiting to see your vision come to pass, be grateful for where you are now. Begin to thank God at this very moment. You are still here in the land of the living. That means there is a divine purpose you have yet to fulfill. This should give you some reason to smile and be happy. Beloved, God is not through with you yet!

Remember Previous Answered Prayers

One way that I try to stay grateful is by remembering the prayers God already answered. There are some things that I used to pray for that I now have. Thank you, Jesus! I constantly remind myself of this daily because I tend to get impatient with God's process. I have all these grand visions and dreams that I believe were given to me by God. Yet, I am impatient at times with the process. I have to remind myself to do what I can, and God will do what I can't do. Also, working on my goals daily helps to keep me grateful, too. This way I am thankful that I even have something to work on.

While penning this chapter, God brought to my remembrance my transition period two years ago. The things I was concerned about then, like moving to a new town, and putting Matthew in a new school, are no longer concerns of mine. As I sit here in my living room, I am filled with gratitude about living in this town and Matthew's school. I am grateful for the wonderful teachers he's had the past two years. I am grateful for my loving and helpful neighbors. I am grateful that I can sleep and wake up in peace. I am also grateful that my ex-husband and I are now peaceful with one another. At one point after the divorce, this was not the case. So, I look back on these things, and I am grateful for all of them. I believe when we have an attitude of gratitude, it allows God to bring more blessings into our lives.

Staying in gratitude also allows you to look beyond what's in the present which may be uncomfortable. This will give you encouragement to move forward. This is another key in being resilient.

Past Hindrances, Future Help

This brings another story to mind that I would like to share. When I was around 3 years old, I had a babysitter who was from Puerto Rico. My parents worked long hours all day long. Maria, my babysitter, talked to me in Spanish. I remember my parents telling me how at one point, I spoke better Spanish than I did English! This may sound great, but when I started Kindergarten, it was a problem.

Before Kindergarten I did not have any previous school experience, it wasn't required then, and my parents said there wasn't a nursery school nearby. So, when I began Kindergarten, the school told my parents that I was having a language difficulty. The school wanted me to receive special services and said I needed help. The school also wanted to conduct some tests because they thought something was wrong with me. I remember my Dad telling me he decided to take me to an outside doctor to get me evaluated. The conclusion from the outside doctor was that there wasn't anything wrong with me, and that I would be just fine. I just needed to *catch up* with the other students. From that day on, my parents worked with me and I began to excel in school. The great thing about being exposed to a second language early in life is that it made me receptive to learning foreign languages.

A Blessing in Disguise

Let's fast forward to this present moment. I am truly grateful that I was taught Spanish at an early age. I cannot even begin to tell you the amount of times I have used it. I am truly so thankful! And, the irony of the whole story is that at that same school, that Spanish might have been a hindrance, it is a blessing now.

I am grateful for learning Spanish, because now I speak it from time to time with the new students. In this school, there is a significant Hispanic population, and some of the new entrants don't speak English. So, guess what? I get to speak Spanish to them. It's so funny how life works, and how God orchestrates things. The very thing that was deemed a hindrance as a child, is now a big help as an adult. Only God can do something like that. Often, we look at our challenges in life as setbacks when they're really setups.

Right now, you may be going through something you don't understand; however, God is setting you up for something greater. Stay in faith, be grateful, and trust the process. *"And we know that God causes everything to work together for the good of those who love God and are called according to His purpose for them" (Romans 8:28 NLT).*

A Love for Reading and Writing

Another thing that came from this was my love for reading and writing. Back then, because my school felt I needed extra help, my parents worked extra hard with me. I recall in third grade reading daily. My Dad would make me read the cover articles on *The New York Times* newspaper. Honestly, back then I thought it was torture. Most of the time, I didn't enjoy it at all. Plus, the words I couldn't pronounce, he would make me look them up in the dictionary. What punishment, I thought! Fast forward to now, I am beyond grateful my Dad pushed me to read not only daily but also included challenging literature. I am a bookworm now because of his persistence and determination. Then in high school, I was a writer for the school magazine. As I look back on all of this, I am grateful.

Staying Grateful

Here are a few ways that can help you with being grateful. The first is to learn to live in the moment. Sometimes, we get ahead of ourselves and try to rush the time and our life away. God has purpose for you each minute of every day. Remember that. Take a minute and breathe in the air. Be thankful for the air you breathe. The place you reside, your family, your children, your job, etc. There are so many things to think about and reflect on. Remember, live in the moment. Appreciate where God has you. *"So, don't worry about tomorrow, for tomorrow will bring its own worries. Today's trouble is enough for today"* (Matthew 6:34 NLT).

Decide to have an attitude of gratitude daily. Remember, the Bible says what you decide on will be done (Job 22:28). How do you decide to have an attitude of gratitude? By filling your mind with God's word, positive affirmations based on His Word, listening to His Word, and reading His Word. Also, I find listening to my favorite pastors preach is another way to keep myself encouraged and grateful.

Nothing changes, unless you do. You can whine, complain all day long but it won't change a thing. You have the power to *make* things happen. As believers, we have been given authority to do so. Guard your mind. Think about what you are thinking about. Don't allow your mind to become a garbage disposal by allowing any junk to enter your mind. It's also necessary to move on the things that God has placed in your heart. Act upon the things you want in life. Always stay grateful for where you are and what God has delivered you from. Remember, where you are now is not your final destination. There is more to come in your life as your latter years will be greater than your former years (Haggai 2:9).

I also make it a point to read literature that is inspirational. My best friend, K. Asher Wilkins, reminds me: "All you need is one paragraph to change your life." Meaning you may read something so simple, that will spark, motivate and compel you to make a change.

My Favorite English Class

I have always loved reading and writing. I remember vividly being in my eighth grade English class with one of my favorite teachers, Mrs. Lind. Oh, how I loved her! She spoke so eloquently that when she spoke you stopped everything to listen. I remember this one time which really stood out to me. She had us enter the room and waited for everyone to be seated. Then she said, "I am going to turn off the lights. I want you to be absolutely silent for five minutes." All the students sat quietly not making a sound. Not even a peep was heard. Once the time had passed, she turned on the lights. Then, she said, "Imagine having to sit quietly for eight hours." We were astonished! Some students exclaimed, "I could never!" She continued, "There was a young girl by the name of Anne Frank that did just that." At the time, none of us knew about Anne Frank. As we later read her story and plight, we knew she was someone remarkable. I will never forget class that day, and the book "The Diary of Anne Frank." It left such an impression on me. I was like, how can a young girl go through so much tragedy and still keep going. I believe it was her resilience as she kept an attitude of gratitude. Towards the end of her diary, Anne Frank said, "In spite of everything I still believe that people are really good at heart."

Being grateful is looking at what you're thankful for and not looking at the negative experiences that has happened to you. Being grateful is having an attitude that what is coming is better than what has been.

Grateful for God's Protection

As an intercessor, I believe I am called to pray for God's protection of those who I love, assigned to pray for, and people in general. One of the great aspects about being a believer is that one of our covenant rights is God's protection. *"God is our refuge and strength, an ever-present help in trouble (Psalm 46:1 NIV)."*

I truly believe that prayer works and that God hears our prayers. Each day when I wake up, I always start my day with prayer. I always pray for God's protection to cover myself and loved ones. I always say, when you pray, you never know what dangers you're protecting yourself from. I also believe that when we pray God's Word and speak it into the atmosphere, angels go to work on our behalf. *"Bless the Lord, you His angels, you mighty ones who do His commandments, obeying the voice of His word"* *(Psalm 103:20 AMP).*

Protection from Hidden Dangers

One day, after dropping my parents at the airport, I went back to their house to pick up a few things I left there. My sister and my son, Matthew, were also with me. I remember driving up the hill, pulling into the driveway, and all of us getting out of the car. I had left the car running, because I planned to quickly go into the house, get what I needed and leave. Well, when I got out of the car, my sister and I started talking, and I decided to turn the car off, so I wouldn't burn gas because the car was idle. That day, it was hot so I had all the windows down. I leaned in through the passenger side of the car, and pushed the ignition button off. Unbeknownst to me, my car was not in park! I thought I put it in park, but the gear was not fully engaged. When I pressed the button off, my car began to slowly roll back down the hill. Instantly, I panicked and went behind the car, moving from side to side thinking I could push it up, (I know, bad idea). I screamed, "Lisa, help!" Then I ran to the driver's side door, hopped in, and slammed my foot on the brake, and finally moved the lever to the park position. My heart was racing so fast, and my palms were sweaty. By that time, Lisa was at the door, and asked, "Are you ok?" Fast forward, today we laugh uncontrollably about it. But, I remember hours after, crying and being so grateful for God's divine protection. So many thoughts flooded my mind. What if I tried to push the car, and my foot got stuck, and the car ran over me? What if Matthew tried to run behind the car and help me? So many scary scenarios ran through my mind. And, the irony of the whole situation was that a few days before, I met with a financial planner discussing my life insurance options and policy. I am thankful for it, but I don't want it to be put to use now! I have more work to do for the Lord. I realize that my work here on earth is not finished. Even now, as I am writing about this, I still have uneasiness about the whole situation. It is amazing because what the enemy means for harm, God will block and protect us from all harm and danger. I can't stop praising God, and being grateful to Him for His protection. I am still here today to tell and write about this story.

Oh, if we can truly grasp how much God loves us. His love is so deep and wide, that our finite minds cannot comprehend it fully. When I think about the many seen and unseen dangers God protects us from, I can't stop praising Him and being grateful for His presence in my life. *"I have loved you, my people, with an everlasting love. With unfailing love, I have drawn you to myself" (Jeremiah 31:3 NLT).*

Keys to Remember

- Everything happens in God's timing
- Be grateful for God's timing

- Be grateful for God's divine purpose for you
- Reflect on previous answered prayers
- A setback is really a setup for something greater
- Be grateful knowing God causes everything to work for your good
- Learn to live in the moment
- Decide to have an attitude of gratitude
- Guard your mind: Think about what you are thinking about
- Be grateful for God's divine protection
- Be grateful for God's unending love

Conclusion

I have learned and still learning in life that there is always a "breakdown before the breakthrough." You may be in a position right now where it seems that your world is falling apart. Just know, as a believer, everything is working for your good. It may seem that things are breaking down, but it is there to build you up for the better. Challenges in life are there to compel us to change. Without the challenges, we would not grow and push past our comfort zone. The pain in life is to push you to a greater purpose. A diamond is only formed when pressure is applied. Give Him the broken pieces of your life and He will turn it into a masterpiece.

I truly believe if you apply the 7 keys I discussed in this book, you will learn how to become resilient. And, then as challenges arise you will know how to face them, and allow them to "bounce" off you. When you realize that everything in life is a process and it happens in stages, you will get to another point of growth. Being resilient, helps you to grow and navigate your way through life. As a believer, our hope and faith is in God. Our trust should be so solid in Him that it does not waver. And, we must keep moving forward in faith daily. This way we will become resilient. "For I am confident of this very thing, that He who began a good work in you will perfect it until the day of Christ Jesus" (Philippians 1:6 NASB).

Salvation Prayer

Father God, I believe that Jesus died for me so that I may have eternal life. I accept Him as my Lord and Savior. Please forgive me of my sins. Come into my heart and show me the right way to live. In Jesus' name, Amen!

www.ingramcontent.com/pod-product-compliance
Lightning Source LLC
Chambersburg PA
CBHW060950040426
42445CB00011B/1096